N

09

10

Twycross

A444

ATHERSTONE

Watling Street

HINCKLE

B4116

A47

A47

A47

NUNEATON

Bedworth

Bulking

M6

A45

COVENTRY

Willenhall

A45

A452

A46

NILWORTH

A445

B4453

LEAMINGTON SPA

A423

WARWICK

A41

A425

Charlecote

A429

Fosse Way

A41

Kineton

B4086

A422

Edge Hill

Tredington

Hornton

Shipston-on-Stour

Compton Wynyates

B4035

BANBURY

A361

Long Compton

in-Marsh

A436

WOLD

Chipping Norton

Gt Tew

A43

B4031

A41

A43

A41

A421

BRACKLEY

A422

BUCKI

LEICESTER

M1

A426

A47

A46

LUTTERWORTH

A427

A427

M6

M45

RUGBY

Dunchurch

Kilsby

M45

A426

A45

A45

DAVENTRY

M1

Southam

Napton

A425

A361

A423

Arbury

Farnborough

A50

A428

A43

A45

NORTHAMPTON

A45

A5

A43

M1

TOWCESTER

A508

A413

A5

A5

England in cameracolour
Warwickshire

England in cameracolour
Warwickshire

PHOTOGRAPHS BY ANDY WILLIAMS

TEXT BY LYNDON F. CAVE

Town
&County
BOOKS

LONDON

A Member of the Ian Allan Group

Bibliography

Warwickshire Villages, Lyndon F. Cave, Robert Hale, 1976
Portrait of Warwickshire, Lyndon F. Cave, Robert Hale (*forthcoming*)
A History of Warwickshire, Terry Slater, Phillimore, 1981
The King's England: Warwickshire, Arthur Mee, Hodder and Stoughton, 1966
The Buildings of England: Warwickshire, ed Nikolaus Pevsner, Penguin
Penguin Guide: Warwickshire, F. R. Banks, Penguin
The Folklore of Warwickshire, Roy Palmer, Batsford, 1976
Warwickshire, Vivian Bird, Batsford, 1973
Warwickshire, Alan Burgess, Robert Hale, 1950

First published 1985

ISBN 0 86364 025 7

Andy Williams ABIPP, AMPA, FRSA, is one of Britain's best known landscape photographers whose work over the last 30 years has given pleasure to thousands in a host of county magazines, numerous calendars and other publications.

Photographs © Andy Williams 1984

© Ian Allan Ltd 1985

Published by Town & County Books , Shepperton, Surrey;
and printed in Italy by
Graphische Betriebe Athesia, Bolzano

Introduction

'Shakespeare's England', 'The Heart of England' and 'Leafy Warwickshire' are all names traditionally associated with Warwickshire and date from the Shakespeare cult of the last century. The birth of Shakespeare was a happy event for the county, but during his lifetime he had little effect on his birthplace. 'Having left little or nothing of his own behind him, he must take a malicious pleasure in the efforts of his townspeople to provide visitors with Shakespeare museums' wrote J. B. Priestley in 1927, then a visitor but until his recent death a famous resident.

Warwickshire is land-locked on all sides, to the north-east by Leicestershire, to the north-west by Staffordshire, by Northamptonshire and Oxfordshire to the south-east and Gloucestershire to the south-west with Worcestershire to the west. The old geographical county, which until 1928 still contained 'islands' of Gloucestershire detached, remained in its historical form until the local government reorganisation of 1974, when a large area of rural central Warwickshire became part of the new administrative county of the West Midlands. Our historic county, sadly mutilated by 20th century politicians, has always been synonymous with 'the centre of England', possessing three claimants to the title; the cross on the village green at Meriden, now in the West Midlands, High Cross on Watling Street, on the northern county boundary, and 'the Midland Oak' which, until it succumbed to old age, stood near Lillington, now part of Leamington Spa, and which has been replaced by one of its progeny.

Warwickshire mostly represents a small scale English countryside typical of what visitors expect of rural England. The natural features are undramatic apart from the Edgehill escarpment on its south-east border, a continuation of the Cotswolds from farther west, but geological changes millions of years ago left isolated hills rising out of the surrounding low land in places such as Napton-on-the-Hill, Claverdon or Nuneaton, recalling the shore-lines of 'Lake Harrison' which in the last Ice-Age covered what is now the Warwickshire Feldon. The lake was named after the modern geologist who established its location, as part of the geological development of the Midlands.

From earlier than the 17th century, historians accepted the division of the county into the Feldon, the prosperous agricultural land south of the Avon valley, and the Arden, which Shakespeare knew as 'the forest of Arden', though much of this ancient woodland on the higher ground north of the Avon had gone by the time he was writing, if indeed it ever existed, and little remains today.

The Feldon was always the farming district, first with medieval open fields spread across the countryside, followed by the inclosures with small hedgelined fields, which in turn are being enlarged to accommodate modern farming techniques requiring large machines. The observant map reader will see that the landscape in the south eastern corner of the county has numerous gaps representing the sites of deserted medieval villages, the casualties of changes in farming during the medieval period and later, and now existing only as names on maps. Probably as many as 130 villages vanished, or shrank to a handful of dwellings or a single farmhouse. Nowadays, the landscape is almost returning to its pre-inclosure appearance where large open fields are essential to the growing of grain and there has been much removal of ancient hedgerows. But the Feldon, from pre-conquest times a farming area, is beginning to change as smaller towns and villages expand, and modern industries replace the traditional ones which relied on farming for their survival. Survival now depends on technological industries and computers, rather than on fields, and less people work on the land and fewer still will need to get mud on their boots.

To the north of the Avon valley, with its low lying sand and gravel deposits, the higher ground, different soils, and in some areas a slightly different climate, have always made life more difficult, and our ancestors had to work harder to thrive in the more barren landscape, which is still discernible in spite of modern farming methods which tend to disguise minor variations in the landscape. Although the area was traditionally known as 'the forest of Arden' this could lead to romantic misconceptions, for unlike the closely forested areas of the New Forest or Sherwood Forest, the Arden was an expanse where dense woodland was interspersed with more open stretches of shrubland, and therefore not good enough to be classed as 'Royal Forest' in the period in which hunting was restricted to the king and his noblemen, taking priority over the needs of the local people.

Settlements such as Henley-in-Arden, Hampton-in-Arden and Tanworth-in-Arden, were carved out of this poorer shrubland and provided timber and foraging for pigs for the more prosperous villages of the Feldon, before the settlements became independent towns in their own right and independent of the more rural south. There are now no extensive woodland areas as in other counties, and the leafy areas are due to planting carried out under landscaping schemes around large country houses built in the 18th or early 19th century. When the houses disappear or are converted to other uses, the trees may be the only reminder of past glories.

Changes are still taking place, for the wealth created by some of the industries of northern Warwickshire, such as mining, now tends to keep the rural Feldon intact regardless of the increasing number of people who would like to retire to its pleasant towns and villages or move as young families with children. It has been suggested that such industry may destroy the Feldon's last chance of surviving as a pleasant countryside, by demanding improved road communications, for the proposed M40 motorway, from Birmingham to Oxford, will take up more of the Feldon's valuable farm land in the process. It has also been suggested, perhaps correctly, that the construction of such a motorway will mean that less through traffic can destroy the character of many of the charming places along its route.

The M40 could be the modern version of the roads which have crossed Warwickshire since Roman times, and perhaps before, and which gave great political power to its landowners. The roads followed earlier trackways, and as laid out by the Romans still carry modern traffic; the Fosse Way, Watling Street and Rykneild Street all traverse Warwickshire. The Fosse Way goes through open countryside, north-east to south-west, almost across the middle of the Feldon and has few settlements on its route. Watling Street, still forming part of the northern county boundary, passes through the old coaching town of Atherstone which developed alongside this important road, now the modern A5, though a by-pass diverts the traffic from its main street. Rykneild Street, running south to north, crosses the Avon at Bidford-on-Avon, a few miles west of Stratford-upon-Avon. After the medieval roads and toll roads were built, the next major road to be constructed in the early nineteenth century, was Telford's road providing the mail coach route from London to Holyhead. Now known as the A45 it follows its original route from London to Daventry, Coventry and Birmingham before turning northwards.

South of the Avon, a series of gradual slopes takes the pleasant and largely unspoilt land up to the Edgehill escarpment, about 500ft above sea level, where Warwickshire's only building stone is found. In a few isolated spots elsewhere in the county, experience has shown that most of these other stones are unsuitable for building purposes, either too hard to cut easily, or crumbling away when exposed to the weather. The few villages perched on, or just below, Edgehill, are of the yellow lias Hornton or Edgehill stone, in character similar to the grey oolite of the Cotswold stone. But descending from Edgehill, to the claylands of the Midland Plain, limestone give place to brick as the predominant building material; pale red brick weathering to an orange colour appears everywhere in central and northern areas, while the small villages and market towns of the south present a pleasantly haphazard mixture of stone and brick buildings in all their streets.

Unlike the Cotswolds, Warwickshire has few complete stone villages, but Warmington, Radway and Tysoe and further from Edgehill, Honington and Cherington, come nearest to the idealised picture, and even here, later brick buildings may be found tucked away among the old stone houses, and more modern intrusions, in materials not found in the immediate vicinity, are uneasily obvious in places where older craftsmen would never have built.

Traditionally, Warwickshire men built in timber framing, with pale red brickwork and roof tiles, which replaced thatch in many places, in turn to be replaced by Welsh grey slates, and in this century, by the ubiquitous concrete tiles. The stone slabs common in Cotswold villages are rare in Warwickshire though a few examples remain in Shipston-on-Stour and the extreme south of the county.

Small in size, great in reputation, slow moving and in places not much more than a mere stream, Warwickshire's Avon runs through the central lowlands and is the county's only direct link with the sea via the Severn and the Bristol Channel. Tourists are drawn by the romantic associations with Shakespeare, but the Avon also draws the naturalists, fishermen, and boating enthusiasts, all with conflicting interests. From Stratford upstream to Warwick is the most untouched section of the river, a haven for wild life, but under pressure from those who see it as a 'highway' whereby larger craft would reach Warwick and continue by canal to other parts of the Midlands, and the battle is still undecided. The river was once essential for the transport of important cargoes from Bristol to Stratford-on-Avon and even in 1745 Defoe in his *Tour throughout the Whole Island of Great Britain* observed that 'the navigation of this river Avon is an exceeding advantage to all this part of the county. . . . For by this river they drive a very great trade for sugar, oil, wine, tobacco, iron, lead and in a word all heavy goods which are carried by water almost as far as Warwick'. Nowadays they drive this very great trade in juggernaut lorries on motorways which cut through the Warwickshire countryside to converge on the well known 'Spaghetti Junction', in part of the Birmingham Conurbation which is still expanding into rural Warwickshire and the neighbouring counties.

But increasing pressure on rural central and northern areas may be outweighed by the environmental changes which must surely take place in the not too distant future when Warwickshire becomes one of the country's new coal mining areas. Vast reserves of high quality coal located under the Kenilworth, Leamington and Warwick district mean that the coal will surely have to be mined eventually, and the impact may make the whole of what was once Shakespeare's countryside into an industrial area inconceivable to Shakespeare or later generations of Warwickshire men.

When the first settlers left the surrounding hills to live in what is now south Warwickshire, the wooded central plain was a very different place. The name of Warwick is related to a settlement of the Hwicce, the earliest reference being to Waerinwican in the Anglo-Saxon chronicle of 1016, and recorded in the Domesday Book of 1086 as Warvic, but in 913, King Alfred's daughter, Ethelfleda Queen of the Mercians, had fortified the tiny hamlet of Warwick at the important river crossing.

When the English shires were formed by the Saxon kings, Warwick became the county town and has remained so. The county became the battleground where Saxons ousted Romano-British, Normans ousted Saxons, the medieval barons fought over it in the Wars of the Roses, and Royalists and Roundheads started the Civil War here, these later battles being to control the river crossings guarded by the castles of Warwick and Kenilworth. The ruins at Kenilworth are evidence of the destruction of the fortifications by Cromwell's troops, but Warwick is still intact.

The first castle on the present site in Warwick was started by William the Conqueror in the best strategic position to control the whole of the Feldon and it is this castle, enlarged and altered, which is the one admired today. Warwick may have shaped English history more than any other castle except the Tower of London and included among its owners the Duke of Gloucester who became Richard III. During the time of 'Warwick the Kingmaker' it was the foremost centre of influence outside the King's court but the age-old association with the Earls of Warwick was broken abruptly in 1980 when the castle was sold and became part of the Madame Tussauds organisation.

Though the most famous of the county families have departed, many of the others have survived the upheavals of the Tudor period and the Civil War by, in some cases, 'keeping their heads down' in times of great political tension, except perhaps for the catholic families like the Throckmortons of Coughton Court, on the losing side when supporting Guy Fawkes and the Gunpowder Plotters.

Nowadays the descendants of these families usually live modestly at home trying to cope with the problems of keeping estates intact and preserving houses which are becoming increasingly valued as part of the national heritage. The county also has many smaller houses of great charm, several hundreds of these still in use, and owned by families of 'yeoman' stock some well-known before Shakespeare's time, such as the Burman family, one of whom ensured a place in history by the accident of being a friend of Anne Hathaway's family.

These houses are in small villages and towns, such as Alcester, Atherstone, Coleshill, Henley-in-Arden, Kineton, Shipston-on-Stour and Southam and all contain buildings of great variety and interest, perhaps reflecting a style different from their neighbours, where the country craftsmen would use whatever was available at hand, timber, stone or brick, following their own fancy, and by their idiosyncracies almost putting their signatures on the locality, an invaluable asset as part of the historical past.

A journey through Warwickshire usually results in the discovery of places associated with Shakespeare, the well-known ones such as his birthplace, New Place, Hall's Croft and the parish church, all in Stratford, or Anne Hathaway's Cottage, Mary Arden's House and Charlecote not far away and other equally authentic but less well-known places to be hunted out by visitors with more time to spare. Many are so familiar as to warrant exclusion from this book which aims to show the less well-known aspects of the 'centre of England', and the towns of importance to Shakespeare and his contemporaries are now overshadowed by Leamington Spa, Rugby, Nuneaton and Bedworth, some of them unknown at the time of Queen Elizabeth I.

Twentieth century Warwickshire has tried to come to terms with vast industrial installations, motorways, and increasing numbers of tourists, and many local people are taking a final look at what was familiar in their youth, so rapid has been the change since 1950, when Alan Burgess, writing on Warwickshire, could call it 'the green core of England'.

Lyndon F. Cave
Leamington Spa 1984

Parish Church at Long Compton The thatched lychgate at the entrance to the church of St Peter and St Paul at Long Compton is well known to all travellers along the A34 which runs through the centre of the village. In fact the lychgate is a cottage, dating from about 1600, with the lower storey removed, partly half-timbered with brick infilling, having been extensively restored after the building was purchased in the early 1950s by Mr Latham, a local builder. In 1964, after Mr Latham's death, his widow handed over the lychgate to the church as a memorial to her husband and it is now used as an entrance to the churchyard, the original entrance being further to the west.

The church is 13th century in date although the tower was built in the following two centuries, but the building as seen today is largely the result of a restoration carried out by the Victorian architect, Mr Woodyer, in 1862-3, which can only be described as drastic. Further restorations followed in 1900 and 1930.

A Rural Landscape near Brailes Sheltered by trees, farm buildings made of local red brick like many of Warwickshire's traditional buildings, stand in a landscape typical of the prosperous farming district of the Feldon in the south of the county. Brailes Hill, rising to 800ft, is a prominent feature of the ancient parish, long established at the time of recording in the Domesday Book. The name may be an old British name for 'a hill with the palace of a chieftain', and as the hill has a steep scarp on all sides it would be a good defensive position. Not far away are the traces of a motte and bailey, possibly constructed by Roger Newburgh, one of the Norman earls of Warwick, to guard the Fosse Way, which runs through the area as it did in Roman times.

The village of Brailes was a bustling market town in the medieval period, the third largest place in the county, whose magnificent parish church dedicated to St George, was known as 'the cathedral of the Feldon'.

10

Fields of Rape, near Shipston-on-Stour
Shipston has long been a market town and was formerly one of the busiest sheep markets in the country. Situated just off the Fosse Way and on the busy road from Oxford to Stratford-upon-Avon and Birmingham, Shipston is the most important settlement in the Feldon, the fertile and gently undulating area south of the Avon, where the lowlands of south Warwickshire begin to rise upwards towards the Cotswold hills. The blazing yellow of the spring-flowering oil seed rape is becoming more characteristic of the landscape than the elms which were once the glory of 'leafy Warwickshire'. Stricken by elm disease, they are now a *memento mori* to the acres of rape.

12

Shipston-on-Stour The town of Shipston increased in importance during the last century being on a long distance stage coach route from London and Oxford to Stratford and Birmingham, and several coaching inns, such as 'The White Bear' and 'The George' seen here, were built in the wide High Street which formed the town's market place. Today these hotels remain in business although the stage coach has given way to the car.

Lying between the Cotswolds and the Midland Plain, Shipston is an attractive mixture of stone and brick houses, many built of local materials and a few still retaining their original roof coverings of stone slabs from quarries found along the Cotswold ridge. The facades of the historic buildings grouped alongside the High Street are mostly 18th and early 19th century in date, although many of these unassuming brick fronts conceal the remains of earlier timber-framed buildings.

14

Tredington This attractive village in the Feldon, is one of the few Saxon settlements in southern Warwickshire. Tredington had hardly changed from the 17th century until the last war, and now it has expanded to become really two separate villages, the original settlement around the village green near the church, and new housing estates on the opposite side of the busy A34 Stratford-upon-Avon to Oxford road. This runs alongside the old village, sandwiched between the road and the river Stour to the east.

The fine stone houses, and rows of smaller brick and stone cottages with thatched roofs, little streets and open spaces make a pleasing pattern, and as the manor originally belonged to the Bishop of Worcester it therefore remained an 'island' of Worcestershire surrounded by Warwickshire, until the county boundaries were altered in the 19th century.

The 200ft spire indicates the location of one of the largest churches in the district, and the only Saxon church in south Warwickshire. The spire of St Gregory's remains a monument to the 15th century, when it was raised on a tower built about a century earlier, which in its turn hides a church of great archaeological and historical interest. The first church on the site was probably built in 961 by Wulston, then Bishop of Worcester, and considerable remains of his Saxon church are still embedded in the work of later generations.

Saxon walls may be seen inside, altered by the Normans and again in 1315 when the church was first consecrated to St Gregory. The last large scale alterations, after those of the 15th century, occurred in 1899 although more work was done recently. Repairs were no doubt needed after the Battle of Edgehill as there are said to be the remains of Royalist bullets in the 14th century door of the north porch. It is a place for all those who admire ancient churches to seek out when visiting south Warwickshire after escaping from the busy tourist centre of Stratford-upon-Avon.

16

Preston-on-Stour An attractive view of an impressive 16th century timber-framed house standing in the centre of Preston-on-Stour, one of the few unspoilt villages in south Warwickshire. On the Alscot Estate, near Stratford-upon-Avon, Preston has been maintained for the last 200 years by the West family, the lords of the manor and owners of the estate, and there has been no new development for over a century until a few years ago when a group of houses was built by Captain West. The village is mostly of Warwickshire red brick, but it has houses of all periods including the late 16th century timber-framed example seen in the photograph, having a close studded ground floor, with square panels above and ornamental infilling of the gables, probably early 17th century in date.

The nearer group of houses were estate dwellings built in 1852, semi-detached and with fish scale tile roofs, 'Tudor' style gables and diamond leaded light windows. These stand not far from the parish church of St Mary, reconstructed between 1752 and 1764, in a mixture of styles resembling the rococo 'gothick' of the nearby manor house at Alscot Park, the home of the West family for several generations. The chancel of the church was altered again in the 19th century and the Rev Harvey Bloom, the rector, in his history of the church dated 1896 wrote 'the chancel looked like a modern railway carriage on a good company's line'.

The River Avon at Welford-on-Avon A pleasant view of the River Avon as it flows through the rural landscape of the Welford-on-Avon district, a stretch of the river which looks untouched, but is in reality dredged and maintained to accommodate large numbers of pleasure craft. This part of Shakespeare's Avon is now controlled by the Lower Avon Navigation Trust, founded in the 1950s by waterway enthusiasts to open up and improve the river to enable boats to travel from the Birmingham area down the Stratford Canal to join the Avon at Stratford and thence down river to the Severn at Tewkesbury and beyond.

This work involved the rebuilding of many locks as well as dredging the river to provide deeper and faster flowing water. When work started it was feared that plant and animal life would suffer from the clearing of vegetation and the possible pollution of the water. It is obvious from this view that despite increasing numbers of boats, parts of the river still retain a tranquil appearance something like the rural scenes which would have been familiar to Shakespeare and succeeding generations.

20

Queen Anne House at Welford-on-Avon A fine example of the 'Queen Anne' houses which can be discovered in many places throughout the Feldon. They indicate the wealth of the farming community during the late 18th and early 19th century and this particular house situated at Welford-on-Avon, is a good example of a mid-18th century house. Two storeys with attic, built in red brick typical of those found throughout the Warwickshire countryside, complete with stone quoins, dressings and moulded keystones. This house of five bays, each complete with its sash window and brick arch over, is distinguished by its prominent central door, with 'gothick' glazing and detached Tuscan columns supporting an enriched curvilinear hood .added at a later date, unlike the plainer door surrounds seen on other houses of this period in the neighbouring villages and small towns.

22

Cottages, Welford-on-Avon Welford itself is now a large village, a few miles west of Stratford-upon-Avon, on a peninsula formed by a loop of the river Avon, a site that the village has occupied since Saxon times. It has attractive groups of old timber-framed and brick cottages, grouped round a village green, but, as in other such villages, all available spaces left as Welford slowly grew during previous centuries, have now been filled in with modern houses as it became a 'dormitory' for Stratford-upon-Avon.

Most of the surviving timber-framed, thatched or tiled cottages, like the group seen here, are 17th century or later in date. All have been extensively modernised to become up-to-date homes for commuters. Cottages and wide grass verges line the minor roads leading away from the village green which is well known for its 70ft high maypole, striped red, white and blue in colour and topped with a fox wind vane. The maypole is not ancient, but is the latest in a long series going back many years, and is used annually when local school children celebrate 'May Day', continuing a custom revived in the last century.

Much of the parish church of St Peter is Norman, although it was largely restored by Sir Gilbert Scott in 1866-7. The lychgate is a modern replica of the original 14th century timber lychgate which became unsafe and was lately removed. The church and the manor estate originally belonged to the Saxon Priory of Deerhurst in Gloucestershire and remained in that county until the boundaries were altered early this century when Welford became part of Warwickshire. The parish church and that of the near-by village of Clifford Chambers both remain in the Diocese of Gloucester.

View from the old bridge at Bidford-on-Avon An attractive view of the Avon from the ancient bridge over the river at Bidford, across which Shakespeare probably walked. Hidden among the trees is the church which he no doubt also visited, although it has been much altered since his time.

In the mid-distance is the site of the ford across the river, indicated by an ancient lane on the east side of the churchyard which stretches down to the riverside. This crossing was used by the Romans travelling along Rykneild Street which runs north to south through the parish, on the line of an old route existing before the Romans came.

Early in the 15th century the ford was replaced by a bridge, first mentioned in 1449 when the Bishop of Worcester offered a year's indulgence to all those contributing to its maintenance. Broken down by Charles I to cover his retreat from Worcester to Oxford and afterwards repaired, it has been restored, as well as widened, in recent years to take heavy modern traffic.

This stretch of the river Avon, in recent years cleared and dredged, attracts many boats making their way downstream to the river Severn at Tewkesbury. From Bidford itself there are views of the pleasant open countryside across the river, towards the distant Cotswolds. The tower of the church of St Lawrence is 13th century, but the original church of the same date was remodelled in the last century. Beyond the church are modern housing estates built on the fringes of the original village founded in the Saxon period.

Cottages at Shottery During Shakespeare's lifetime, and up to the last century, Shottery was a separate village a short distance to the west of Stratford-upon-Avon, but the built-up area of the modern borough has now engulfed it. Between the wars housing developments closed the gap between the two places and after the last war when further expansion took place beyond Shottery itself, all available space in the village centre was filled in with new houses. Shottery stands preserved between these two new estates, perhaps unobserved by those visitors who seek Anne Hathaway's Cottage. What makes the difference is that today the surroundings have changed beyond recognition from what Shakespeare knew, with over-restored houses, souvenir shops, and a coach park near the ancient church. The village is now suburbanised, although a few old cottages, such as the group shown in this photograph, survive in spite of everything else.

Such well-preserved half-timbering, thatched roofs and white painted walls, are to be found near the village green. These date from the 16th or 17th centuries, the large timber-framed panels being typical of the period when timber was becoming scarcer than in the previous centuries. Originally the wood, always oak or elm, would have been left its natural colour as would the brickwork, or wattle and daub infill, but the present black and white is a fashion which appealed to the Victorians and remained popular in our own period.

28

Anne Hathaway's Cottage, Stratford-upon-Avon Anne Hathaway was the daughter of William Hathaway who died a year before Anne married William Shakespeare. Anne, born in 1556 or 1557, married William in 1582 being eight years older than her husband. After her father's death Anne, then 26, lived on in Hewland's Farm with her stepmother and three stepbrothers; this cottage, the property of the Shakespeare Birthplace Trust, has been known as Anne Hathaway's Cottage since 1795, but in fact was never her property, being always owned by her stepmother.

The cottage is a timber framed building with a thatched roof and latticed windows, typical of what the visitor expects of a small house of the Elizabethan period. The build-ing was originally hardly a cottage, being a spacious twelve-roomed farmhouse and the earliest parts date from some time in the 15th century. The external walls are timber-framed with wattle and daub or brick infill to the panels while inside is a pair of curved crucks supporting part of the roof. The central chimney stack was rebuilt in 1697 and bears the initials of John Hathaway; whose descendants lived in the house until 1892, when the property was purchased by the Birthplace Trust, the first to be acquired after the Birthplace itself.

Since that time the building has been extensively restored and in particular in 1969 when a fire started by an arsonist destroyed the thatched roof and its support-ing timbers as well as doing considerable damage to the interior and its contents. Fortunately the most important furniture was saved including the famous carved bedstead which belonged to the Hathaway family for many generations, as well as the settle where Anne and Shakespeare are said to have done their courting.

Hall's Croft, Stratford-upon-Avon   Hall's Croft, in Old Town, Stratford-upon-Avon, once the home of Shakespeare's daughter Susanna and her husband, John Hall, is now owned by the Shakespeare Birthplace Trust. It was purchased in 1949, the last of the properties in the town associated with Shakespeare and his family to be acquired by the Trust. In 1607 John Hall, a local physician, married Susanna and they lived in the house until Shakespeare's death in 1616 after which they moved to New Place. John Hall practised his profession from the house, which did not become known as Hall's Croft until long after his death.

John Hall, apart from being Shakespeare's son-in-law, is known for his book *Select Observations on English Bodies* published in 1657 and written in Latin. It was translated into English after his death by a fellow physician and contains prescriptions for such things as a poultice made of 'swallow's nest, dirt, dung and all the contents boiled in chamumel and lilies to which was added a white dog's turd, one ounce of meal, of linseed and foena greek, ointment of Diathea and hen's grease each half an ounce and apply hot to make a poultice'. Susanna's epitaph describes her as 'Witty above her sex, but that's not all, Wise to salvation was good Mistress Hall'.

Hall's Croft is not far from the parish church where John Hall and his wife are buried near the famous dramatist and is a good example of a spacious Tudor house, with some 17th century and later additions. It is 'L' shaped with a close studded timber framed ground floor built on a stone base and over hanging upper floors with square shaped framed panels typical of the construction of the period, filled in with lath and plaster; the porch is not original.

New Place, Stratford-upon-Avon The garden of New Place marks the site of the house built about 1485 by Sir Hugh Clopton, who became Lord Mayor of London in 1480. He also built the 14-arched bridge over the Avon in 1490, which is known as the Clopton Bridge and is still used nearly 500 years later. The house was on the corner of Chapel Street near the Guild Chapel, part of which Hugh Clopton also rebuilt in 1492. New Place was purchased for £60 from William Underhill by Shakespeare in 1597 and it was where he retired probably to write his later plays, dying there at the age of 52 on 23 April 1616.

The Deed of Sale showed that in addition to the house there were also two barns and a large garden with an orchard, but no mention was made of the mulberry tree under which Shakespeare is supposed to have sat. At his death the house passed to his daughter Susanna and her husband Dr John Hall, and then to their daughter Elizabeth, who lived there with her husband Thomas Nash and, after he died, with her second husband John Bernard. Elizabeth was the last of Shakespeare's direct descendants and on her death in 1675 the house was sold.

The new owner, Sir Edward Walker, altered the house early in the 18th century, giving it a brick front in keeping with the fashion of the time, after which it was brought by Rev Francis Gastrell who was so annoyed by the number of people asking to see the mulberry tree associated with Shakespeare that he cut it down to the fury of the townspeople. The wood was made into all sorts of curios which were sold to visitors of the time. In 1759 Gastrell had a further quarrel about the payment of the parish rate for maintaining the poor, with the result that he declared that New Place should never pay any rates again and demolished the house. He then left Stratford among 'the rages and curses of the inhabitants' although by then the much altered house had little resemblance to the one owned by Shakespeare. Sixteen years later his widow sold the site of the house and it has never been built on since. Nothing remains but part of the foundations and the site has been laid out with gardens.

Royal Shakespeare Theatre, Stratford-upon-Avon A dramatic view of the Royal Shakespeare Theatre seen in the evening across a placid river Avon which once supported a flotilla of swans, now sadly deserted because of lead poisoning or other disasters. The Memorial Theatre, to give the theatre its original name, is the second to stand on this site; the first was built in 1879 in an odd Victorian 'gothic' style of red brick with light coloured stripes of brick and stone with odds and ends of half timbering dotted around. This was burnt down in 1926 although the wing which now contains the library and art gallery survived and can still be seen next to the present building.

The Royal Shakespeare Theatre is by Miss Elizabeth Scott, a great niece of the famous Victorian architect Sir Gilbert Scott, and she won the open competition held for its design. The new theatre was opened in 1932 by the Prince of Wales, later Edward VIII. At the time it aroused a great deal of criticism because of its cube-like structure of red brick typical of much of the architecture of the period. It has been altered and extended with a new stage tower, and a new riverside elevation has been created by the enlargement of the restaurants. The interior has also been completely remodelled to provide more seating accommodation and to allow for changes in theatrical ideas with the result that the only parts in their original form are the entrance hall and the main staircase. The theatre has been used for presenting the plays of Shakespeare from mid-April to October since it was opened, and in 1961 the name was changed to the Royal Shakespeare Theatre.

Perhaps the theatre at night is best described by T. C. Kemp, when he was the drama critic of *The Birmingham Post*, 'Look downstream and you will see the lighted theatre hanging motionless over the water, a glittering galleon to the north of the town outlined in ebony against a fading sky'.

Town Centre, Stratford-upon-Avon This attractive group of buildings in the town centre welcomes visitors as they approach up Bridge Street, the main street leading from the river Avon and the Clopton Bridge to Henley Street and Shakespeare's Birthplace. It is a route used for centuries as Bridge Street is in fact the Romano-British road to the original ford over the Avon.

The view is often thronged with traffic negotiating the floral displays which form a feature of the roundabout at this busy road junction. The bank and its prominent clock tower dominates the corner of Wood Street, Henley Street and Bridge Street, and was built in 1821 by William Thompson. The building was originally the market house occupying then, as now, one of the most important sites in the town although more hidden from the onlooker than nowadays as Bridge Street then had a row of buildings down its centre, where today rows of cars are parked.

Some of the timber-framed buildings seen in the photograph are old properties largely remodelled in the last century, and more recently, to create the half-timbered frontages considered more in keeping with the character of the town than those originally on the site. This 'Elizabethan' style was largely created by stripping the 18th and 19th century brick and plaster fronts from the existing buildings and replacing them with timber-framing; a fashion encouraged by Marie Corelli, the romantic novelist who spent the last years of her life in Stratford-upon-Avon.

The gentle curve of Henley Street, seen to the right of the photograph, leads the visitor around the corner to the most visited building in the town — Shakespeare's Birthplace.

Charlecote Park, Wellesbourne Charlecote Park, on the banks of the Avon six miles south of Warwick and four miles east of Stratford-upon-Avon, has belonged to the National Trust since 1946 and is visited by almost all those who come to explore the Shakespeare country.

The 200 acres of parkland surrounding the house were laid out in the 18th century by the famous landscape gardener, Capability Brown, and still support a large herd of deer, as in the time when the young Shakespeare was reputed to have gone poaching in the park.

The present house, replacing an older one on the site, was started by Sir Thomas Lucy in 1551 and was 'E' shaped, typical of the period, and while the porch and wings are original most of the remainder of the 'Elizabethan' house was built or altered in the 19th century. Sir Thomas was knighted in 1565, 'dubbed in his own house', and traditionally is thought to have been satirically portrayed as Justice Shallow in *The Merry Wives of Windsor*.

The house contains a magnificent collection of stained glass and furniture designed by Thomas Willement between 1823 and 1845, with later works by John Gibson, as well as many pictures and a fine library containing nearly 3,000 volumes. Many of the works of art were purchased by the Lucy family at the sale of William Beckford's collection at Fonthill Abbey early in the last century.

The gatehouse, seen here in front of the house, is however a genuine Elizabethan building, approached along an elm avenue sadly ravaged by disease, though losses are being made good by planting other species of young trees. Queen Elizabeth I passed through the gatehouse when she visited Charlecote in 1572, and present day visitors still approach the house by the same way. The gatehouse has remained unaltered, its red brick matured to an attractive rose pink, with grey stone dressings, square shaped, with a flat roof surrounded by a stone balustrade with rosette motifs. But the polygonal angle turrets with ogee caps give the building its unique character; above the rounded archway and vaulted entrance passage is a fine oriel window, and the flagpole flies the National Trust flag on open days and the family flag when the family is in residence.

Mary Arden's House, Wilmcote Mary Arden's House is the house traditionally associated with Shakespeare's mother although she never owned the house but lived there as the daughter of Robert Arden, a yeoman farmer in the neighbourhood. The property was bought by her grandfather in 1501 and Mary lived there until her marriage to John Shakespeare about 1557. Although in later years it had been split up into cottages, the house was used as part of a working farm until 1930 when it was purchased by the Shakespeare Birthplace Trust. It was first called Mary Arden's House in 1798, but as recently as 1914 W. H. Hutton writing in *Highways and Byways in Shakespeare's Country* said 'you see three cottages (or they seem to be) which were

the farmhouse in which Mary Arden, perhaps, was born. They have dormer windows set in the roof and the eastern end with its old beams is picturesque. But for the rest the house has no great claim to a visit. Shakespeare's mother lived here as a girl, that is all. Perhaps it is enough'.

Since then all has changed, the house being extensively, but beautifully restored by the Birthplace Trust. It consists of a long range facing the road, opposite the village green, and has a gabled wing at the east end. The main house has vertical close-studded timber framing on both floors while the wing, a later addition, has herringbone timbering on the front with open squares of timber framing on the side wall; the whole house is on a stone plinth.

It has a simple plan with the front door opening on to a cross passage, to the left the kitchen and on the right the original hall, which was open to the roof; this has had a later floor inserted dividing it into two floors. Off the hall is a dairy with a single room on the ground floor of the wing, from which the staircase leads to the bedrooms connected to each other. There is a fine collection of antique furniture acquired by the Trust as no furniture descended with the house. The kitchen contains old kitchen appliances and domestic ware in keeping with the period of a house of this style.

Behind the house is the former farmyard and outbuildings, also timber framed, as well as an old dovecote with boxes for about 650 doves.

42

La Tete de Boeuf, at Wootton Wawen A view of the 'La Tete de Boeuf', formerly 'The Bull's Head', an old posting house at Wootton Wawen, typical of the many half-timbered houses and inns to be found throughout the county. It was originally two cottages and stables with some timber-framing dating from the Middle Ages although the building was extensively altered during the last 200 years. While the date 1597 found on the building is open to question it does not detract from the popularity of the inn.

The large heavy square timber-framing is typical of any time between the 17th and 18th centuries, and a fair amount of the original appearance is retained externally although little of the old interior remains. The dormer windows are of later date, with typical late 19th century carved bargeboards.

Wootton Wawen, a Saxon 'farm by the wood' was founded in 723 AD and the actual deed granting the land has survived to become one of the treasures of the British Museum. The village lies to the south of Henley-in-Arden on the old stage coach route between Stratford-upon-Avon and Birmingham, still crowded with vehicles. The older buildings lie alongside the main road, evidence of the age of this approach to the crossing of the Avon at Stratford.

The village is dominated by one of the most interesting churches in Warwickshire, one of the few to contain Anglo-Saxon work. The oldest part of the building, the Saxon sanctuary, is still used as a chapel and elsewhere in the church can be seen remains of Norman work as well as many features from the 12th to the 15th centuries.

Packwood House, Hockley Heath A glimpse of Packwood House across a daffodil field. The house, now the property of the National Trust is partly hidden behind the forecourt on the north side of which is a range of brick buildings, built about 1660, and on the other side is the enclosed Carolean Garden with its four gazebos. The house is perhaps best known for its topiary garden whose clipped yews represent the Sermon on the Mount, the trees being of varying ages, some planted in the last century. The Multitude Walk, a long line of conical yews, leads to a raised walk bordered by twelve great yews — the Apostles — in the centre of which stand four even larger trees — the Evangelists, and crowning the top of the mount, ascended by a spiral path, is a single giant yew.

From the 15th century until 1869 the house was owned by the Fetherston family, and General Ireton, one of Cromwell's officers, is said to have slept here before the Battle of Edgehill in 1642. The original house was a timber-framed building of about 1560, rendered over in the 18th century, and almost unchanged until it was acquired by the Ash family in 1905. The house has now been enlarged and drastically altered so the original house is almost unrecognisable, refurbished by Mr Baron Ash between 1925 and 1937, when he collected plasterwork, panels, stained glass, fireplaces and fittings from many sources. During this period the Great Hall was formed out of an old cruck barn, linked to the house by a 1930's long gallery complete with pictures and tapestries.

Packwood, furnished with fine pieces of 17th and 18th century furniture collected by Mr Ash, was presented by him to the National Trust early in the last war and is now open to the public at varying times during the year.

46

Baddesley Clinton House, near Hockley Heath Baddesley Clinton House, one of the gems of the Warwickshire countryside, is the most perfect of all the late medieval semi-fortified manor houses still surviving in the Midlands. The original house was built in the 15th century by John Brome, remained in the Brome family until 1517 when it passed, by marriage, to Sir Edward Ferrers. His descendants held it until 1884 when it passed to a distant branch of the family who took the name Ferrers-Walker. A few years ago a member of the family presented the property to the National Trust, ensuring that this unique house was saved for posterity.

Baddesley Clinton House stands in a secluded setting not far from the National Trust property, Packwood House, and near the house is the parish church of St Michael, a fine example of a small country church largely dating from the 13th century. The manor house and church form the centre of a parish which contains remnants of Hay Wood, the 'enclosed wood' of Saxon times, about 200 acres in extent and perhaps the last survivor of the ancient forest of Arden. The site of the original deserted medieval village is near the manor house, away from the present village which is some distance from the house and church near the modern road to Birmingham.

The entrance front of this ancient stone house with its porch, oak door and contemporary ironwork, was built about 1459 and is approached by a Queen Anne brick bridge, replacing the old drawbridge across the moat which surrounds the whole building. Above the entrance is a great six light window, a later alteration, which with other work of the late 16th and early 17th centuries was undertaken for Henry Ferrers, the antiquarian who provided Dugdale with much material for his famous history, and who died in 1633.

Town Hall, Birmingham A view of the Town Hall, Birmingham, standing almost alone among the newer buildings of the city centre, and recently cleaned of ancient smoke and grime, an operation made worthwhile thanks to the smoke control regulations covering most of the city. Modelled on the Temple of Castor and Pollux in the Roman Forum, and built of brick faced with Anglesey marble, it was designed in 1832 by J. A. Hansom and Edward Welch, then unknown architects who were made to stand surety for the builder. Because too low an estimate for the work was submitted the builders, as well as the architects, were declared bankrupt in 1834. The work continued under Charles Edge and the building was not completely finished until 1861. It is 150ft long by 65ft wide, with 42 columns each 36ft high mounted on a stone base which provides accommodation under the first floor concert hall. The interior is one large assembly hall, in the Georgian tradition, and originally had one gallery until a second one was added during internal alterations carried out in 1927.

The concert hall was chosen for the first performance of Mendelssohn's *Elijah* and Elgar's *Dream of Gerontius*. Joseph Aloysuis Hansom later designed many Roman Catholic churches and also the cathedral of SS Mary and Boniface in Plymouth, completed in 1858. But he is probably best known for his design of 'The Patent Safety Cab', patented by him in 1842 and popularly called 'The Hansom Cab'.

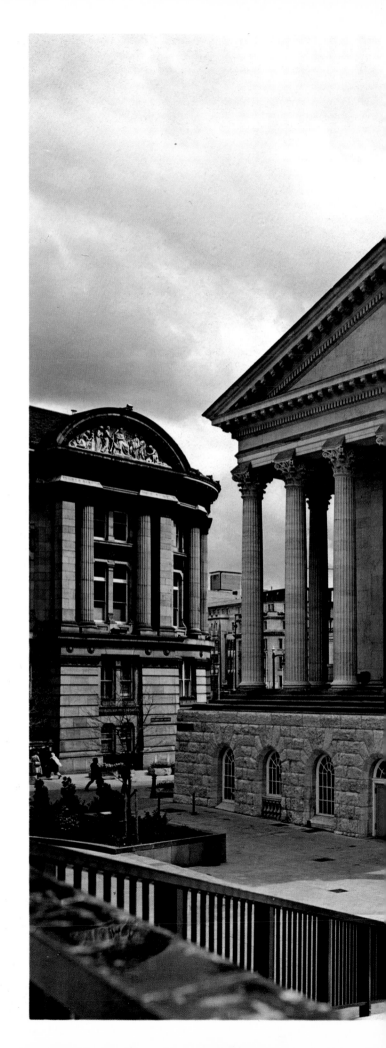

Gas Street Canal Basin, Birmingham In spite of its unpromising name, Gas Street Canal Basin is a surprisingly interesting area hidden away behind Gas Street and Broad Street almost in the centre of Birmingham and unknown to many people who daily pass along the crowded city streets.

It is at the hub of the Birmingham canal system and is the site of the original junction between the Birmingham and Worcester canals constructed about 1769, which for many years were separated by a 'bar' due to the rivalry of the two companies who refused passage to each other's boats.

It was originally surrounded by warehouses, many now demolished but some of the original buildings survive as can be seen at one end of the basin which now houses a colony of narrow boats. Many of these were old working boats now used for residential or pleasure purposes.

In 1967 the City of Birmingham improved the area to make it into an open space and a marina for boats, building a waterside public house and several blocks of flats to create new life around an area of water important in a city lacking a large river.

52

The Rotunda, Birmingham The Rotunda, the tall cylindrical building now familiar to visitors to Birmingham, is in strong contrast to the rectangular neighbouring buildings and has become the 'trade mark' of the post-war redevelopment of the Victorian city centre. This building with its 24 floors of commercial premises, built in 1964-5 to the designs of James Roberts, has been described by Pevsner as 'a splendid design for its position' a view not shared by every Birmingham citizen, although its appearance now causes less controversy than when it was first built, nearly 20 years ago.

It stands at the top of the hill above the Bull Ring at the junction of New Street and High Street, and towers 271ft above the Ringway. The Bull Ring, traditionally the old market place of the City, is now mostly covered by the Shopping Centre, built in the early 1960s, but a corner survives as an open air market whose colourful stall canopies can be glimpsed beyond the Ringway, unusually quiet in this view, generally being jammed with city traffic. The Rotunda, standing at a focal point in the web of urban motorways, lends Birmingham an air suggestive of a North American city rather than that traditionally associated with a great English centre of industry.

54

Meriden By long tradition the Centre of England, Meriden was, until 1974, part of the historic County of Warwick but it is now part of the administrative West Midlands County. The change is even now not welcomed, the historic links of the village having been with Warwickshire ever since the county came into existence.

Old and new buildings, including the Centre of England post office, form an attractive surround to the village green, for many years the property of the lord of the manor, the Earl of Aylesford, who lives at nearby Packington Hall, although the green is now owned by the parish.

On the green is what remains of the 500 year-old sandstone cross marking the actual Centre of England, and beyond it is the obelisk erected as a memorial to those cyclists who died on active service in both world wars. A service of remembrance is held here annually on a Sunday in May, but the numbers attending dwindle year by year.

The village is now rather quieter than it was, since the by-pass opened in 1958 has taken away much of the traffic which thundered through the village along the A45, the old mail coach route from London to Holyhead which in recent years had taken increasing numbers of heavy lorries. In 1745, on Meriden Heath, the Duke of Cumberland set up his headquarters while attempting to block the Young Pretender's advance to London. Meriden is also the headquarters of England's oldest archery society formed in 1788, but in existence before then, the Woodmen of Arden, whose membership has by tradition always been limited to 80 archers with the Earl of Aylesford as its hereditary president.

Kenilworth Castle About 1125 Geoffrey de Clinton, Treasurer and Chief Justice of England, established a castle at Kenilworth worthy of his office, but it was financed, coveted and finally acquired by the Plantagenet Kings. It became a royal castle, the home of earls, the prison of royalty, and a place of lavish entertainment for Queen Elizabeth I, who had given it to her favourite Robert Dudley, Earl of Leycester, in 1564. John of Gaunt had built his part of the castle with dignity and strength, but Robert Dudley added more ranges of buildings and 'improved' some of the Norman features with fashionable Tudor modernisation intended to please Elizabeth. The remains of the 12th century keep still tower above the rest of the ruins outlined against the skyline and seen by all travellers approaching Kenilworth from the north. The keep was built in 1170-1180 by John of Gaunt, who made the castle his stronghold during the Wars of the Barons, but it suffered under the attacks of the Parliamentarians in the Civil War several centuries later.

The photograph shows the ruins of the castle, from the west, across the site of the 'mere', a large defensive lake outside the perimeter walls, where water pageants were also provided for the enjoyment of Elizabeth I. The Pleasance, on the north side of the castle, was also laid out for use as a pleasure garden during the visit of Elizabeth to the castle; within a few centuries the magnificence had vanished, the castle being 'slighted' by Cromwell and becoming an uninhabitable ruin while the mere drained away leaving the red sandstone walls defenceless.

During the last century the castle was a romantic ivy covered ruin admired by writers, such as Sir Walter Scott whose novel *Kenilworth* is loosely based on the history of the fortress, while Nathanial Hawthorne wrote 'without the ivy and shrubbery this huge Kenilworth would not be a pleasant object'. It was the property of the Earl of Clarendon until 1937 when it was purchased by Sir John Siddeley, later Lord Kenilworth, came into the care of the Office of the Works, succeeded by the Department of the Environment who still look after the ruins. The 2nd Lord Kenilworth formally presented the castle to the town of Kenilworth in 1958, the 400th Anniversary of the accession of Elizabeth I to the throne.

58

Mill Street, Warwick A view of the houses in Mill Street, outside the old town walls and therefore escaping the ravages of the fire of 1694. The street runs down to the base of the massive perimeter walls and defensive towers of the castle, and the remains of the original water mill on the banks of the river Avon. The mill has long since ceased to exist, but the street with its attractive timber-framed and brick-fronted houses, has become one of the most sought after residential areas in present day Warwick.

Almost all the houses were originally built between the 15th and 17th centuries and although extensively altered internally many retain their original timber framed fronts, while others were cased with brickwork in the later 18th or early 19th centuries when the 'Georgian' style with its sash windows became fashionable.

A group of these houses is shown in the photograph and beyond them a magnificent range of timber framed houses lines the street as it curves down to the river Avon. Among these timber framed houses are two altered Wealden type houses, built about 1500, originally with jettied fronts, and the Mill House built in the mid-15th century, and restored in the early years of this century. Its heavy exposed joists and close set studding form an attractive frontage at the end of the street, while Allen's House, the largest house built before 1600, was built by Tomas Allen in MDLXVIII (1568) according to the date stone set into the facade. Although much altered, its close set studs are still visible concealing the remains of an old three bay house, the central bay originally being a hall open to the roof with service rooms and parlours in the two end bays.

What probably first attracts the attention of visitors is the elaborate ornamental bracing of the central group of houses built in the last century in the 'New Elizabethan' style popular with the Victorians and still generally admired nearly a century later.

Church Street, Warwick Church Street, Warwick, leads up to the tower of St Mary's, the town's ancient parish church, one of whose unique treasures is the Beauchamp Chapel.

The four principal streets of the medieval town met at a cross roads where there was a market cross, long since disappeared. Church Street led from the cross to the church and was traditionally the site of the barley market, and like other streets in the town, was bordered with old timber-framed houses, until the fire of 1694 destroyed most of the centre of Warwick. One of the few buildings to survive was the Beauchamp Chapel, although the rest of the church was burnt down.

Rebuilding followed the fire, and many of the brick fronted early 18th century houses have slightly older timber-framed buildings behind the front brick walls. Church Street has changed little in appearance since the mid-19th century except for the insertion of shop-fronts in the ground floor of some of the houses.

In 1698, the rebuilding of the church tower was started, and it was planned to stand on the west wall of the church and two piers inside the nave, but when the tower had risen to 26ft above the walls, it was found to be unsafe. It was taken down and in 1700 rebuilt over the roadway, one of the few church towers in this country to be built over a public thoroughfare and traffic passed through the arches under the tower, until this was prohibited after the last war.

The church was finished in 1704, the tower rising to 174ft to the top of the pinnacles which were replaced by William Butterfield in 1885. The tower, in perpendicular gothic style was built to the designs of Sir William Wilson of Sutton Coldfield, traditionally with advice from Sir Christopher Wren, but more probably from Wren's master mason Edward Strong. It has recently been restored and cleaned, its decayed stonework replaced and the shields at the top newly painted. Remains of the original clock are preserved in the church, but the modern clock, whose chimes play popular late-Victorian ballad tunes at intervals during the day, was made by Smith of Derby in 1903.

Lord Leycester Hospital, Warwick The Lord Leycester Hospital is one of the oldest buildings in Warwick, a magnificent range of timber-framed buildings which stands on a raised stone terrace, adjacent to the west gate of the town, the point from which this photograph was taken. The approach is through a stone arched gateway over which is the inscription *Hospitivm Collegiatvm Roberti Dvdlei Comitis Leycestriae* flanked by the date 1571, with the Dudley device, a double tailed lion rampant, in the left spandrel and the Sidney device, a pheon or barbed dart, in the other. The buildings are now open to the public.

In the Middle Ages the hall, which forms part of the Hospital, was owned by the United Guilds of the Holy Trinity, the Blessed Virgin and St George the Martyr, established in 1383. In 1546 the Guilds were dissolved by Henry VIII and the buildings passed to the Burgesses of Warwick until 1571, when Queen Elizabeth's favourite Robert Dudley, Earl of Leycester, signified his desire that the buildings should be given him for use as a hospital or almshouses for old soldiers who had served in the regiments raised in the district, in particular the Gloucestershire, Leicestershire and Warwickshire regiments.

The foundation charter allowed for twelve Brethren and a Master and it has provided a home for ex-Servicemen ever since. Originally accommodation was only for unmarried men or widowers, but since the 1960s the buildings have been divided into flats for married couples so that old soldiers and their wives may spend the rest of their lives in these ancient surroundings. The Brethren must attend church regularly as required by the original charter and wear a special costume of Elizabethan hats, black cloaks and silver badges, which are the original Elizabethan ones except for one which replaced a badge lost many years ago. The costume is worn on Sunday, or on other ceremonial occasions, for services in the ancient chapel of St James, which is perched over the West Gate.

Over the entrance to the courtyard is 'The Bear and Ragged Staff' a device associated with the Earls of Leycester and later Warwickshire itself, now the crest of the County Council. Grouped around the courtyard are the old Guildhall, the Master's House, and the Dining Hall where Sir Fulke Greville entertained James I when he visited Warwick in September 1617.

Beauchamp Chapel, St Mary's Church, Warwick The Beauchamp Chapel is one of the glories of Warwickshire. It was built at a cost of £2,481 4s 7½d between the years 1442 and 1462 in accordance with the will of Richard Beauchamp, Earl of Warwick, who died at Rouen in 1439. It is considered by many to be the finest chantry chapel in the country and the best example of the perpendicular style, apart from the Henry VII Chapel at Westminster Abbey and King's College Chapel at Cambridge. It was built to house the superb monument to the Earl of Warwick, father of 'The Kingmaker', which is seen in the centre of the photograph.

The chapel has elaborately panelled stone walls of three bays with a cusped octagonal panel in the centre of each fan vault with the lierne vaulting divided by ribs with carved stone bosses at the intersections. The view shows the east window with stonework tracery on either side decorated with canopied saints and angels, all re-coloured during the recent restoration. Each figure bears a musical instrument, providing in stone an almost complete collection of the instruments in favour at that time. These unusual carvings represent some of the best mid-15th century sculpture in the country, while the glass in the window is also highly prized. The glass was made by the Royal Glazier, John Pruddle of Westminster, and remnants of this ancient glass dating from 1441 are incorporated in the east window. The upper parts of the side lights contain contemporary figures, but the window is above all celebrated for its example of 15th century musical notation represented as a long scroll carried through the tracery lights, though the south, or right hand side, of the glass is not original.

The reredos of 1735 replaces the one destroyed by the Parliamentary forces in 1642, and the 'gothick' canopied carved panel is flanked by medieval stonework. The Earl's monument has a life-like effigy of gilded brass mounted on a Purbeck marble tomb chest, the sides enriched with 14 gilded brass 'weepers', figures representing members of the Earl's family, with 'The Kingmaker' on the south side. The Earl is shown in plate armour, head resting on a helmet, hands raised in prayer, with muzzled bear and a griffin at his feet.

Warwick Castle The almost impregnable fortifications of Warwick Castle are seen in a dramatic view of Caesar's Tower taken from outside the defensive walls rising out of the solid rock face at the end of Mill Street.

The tower was built for Thomas Beauchamp the elder, who died in 1369 and in the 17th century had acquired the name of Poitiers Tower, because prisoners taken at the Battle of Poitiers by the Earl of Warwick were imprisoned in the base of the tower, their ransoms paying for the strengthening of the castle fortifications.

The tower rises to 147ft, and was built at a time when English military architecture had reached its peak of perfection. It is part of a castle among the few in the country never taken by direct assault. Begun in the Norman period and extended in following centuries, the castle is also among the few to survive the Civil War without major damage. From the restoration until recent times, it has been a residence for the Earls of Warwick and their families.

Caesar's Tower is of an irregular quatrefoil shape on a deep battered base rising out of the rock face. The base of the tower holds a vaulted dungeon to which a long flight of steps descends from the castle courtyard. The three floors above have rooms with stone vaulted ceilings, later windows cut through the walls, and 17th century fireplaces, and at the top a guard room and a parapeted platform leading to the parapet walk around the perimeter walls.

According to a survey of 1590, the tower was already in decay at that date, and the process of repair has been going on intermittently ever since. The buildings next to the tower were improved from the 18th century onwards, when the castle became a domestic dwelling, and beyond them are the towers of the gatehouse and barbican, with Guy's Tower rising in the background, above the main defensive walls.

The Earls of Warwick controlled, and later owned, the castle since the time of the Normans but in 1980 it was sold to Madame Tussauds, who have continued the long established practice of opening the castle and its treasures to the public throughout the year.

Town Hall, Leamington Spa A view of the Town Hall which dominates the Parade and is the largest Victorian building to be erected on the main street of this Regency spa town. The Parade, built between 1810 and 1830 is still the principal shopping street, although the original dwelling houses of the Regency period have been drastically altered by the insertion of later shop fronts or replaced by the ubiquitous new commercial buildings.

The foundation stone of the Town Hall was laid on 18 October 1882 and it was opened two years later on 18 September 1884. It was erected among the earliest buildings of the Parade, those opposite originally dating from between 1810 and 1815. Just beyond the Town Hall is the corner of the Regent Hotel which when built in 1819 was reputed to be the largest hotel in Europe, being named after the Prince Regent whose coat of arms appears over one of the entrances.

The statue of Queen Victoria seen here is typical of many erected in honour of her Diamond Jubilee and the obelisk was placed at the end of Holly Walk in 1880 in honour of Henry Bright by whose efforts a free public water supply for the town had been achieved two years earlier.

Jephson Gardens, Leamington Spa The Jephson Gardens, in the centre of Royal Leamington Spa, were laid out in 1834 on the north bank of the River Leam on land which was leased to the town by Edward Willes, who then owned much of the area east of the Parade, the main street of the Regency spa. His lease stipulated that the land should not be built on, and later in the 19th century the site was bought by the town, and since 1974 has been under the control of the Warwick District Council.

The obelisk was placed in the gardens in honour of Edward Willes after his death, but not until 1875, long after the gardens first opened to the public.

They were first called the Newbold Gardens, but in 1845, after enlargements and improvements as a public testimonial to Dr Jephson, the name was changed and the newly designed gardens opened on 12 May 1846. Since then the gardens have remained intact, the area being unchanged since the ground was first laid out and the planting of trees and shrubs has continued, except for a period during the last war.

The 13 acres of gardens contain a lake and two fountains modelled on those at Hampton Court, as well as beautiful floral displays. As the gardens were originally planned as an arboretum, many of the young trees planted then are now mature, and make a fine collection, with examples of unusual species not normally grown in this country.

Dr Jephson came to Leamington in 1828 and continued his medical practice until blindness necessitated his retirement about 1848, and he died 30 years later. Dr Jephson, more than any other medical practitioner of the time, was responsible for making Leamington famous for its health cures based on the abundant supply of spa water from the mineral springs. His patients included many well known people, among them Ruskin, but he also did much charitable work among the poor, helping to improve sanitary conditions in the town, and with others, working to establish the local hospital, which still exists.

The Pump Rooms, Leamington Spa
Beyond the entrance lodges of the Jephson Gardens which were built in 1846, although the memorial gates are modern, can be seen the Pump Rooms. These were built, after the discovery of a spring in 1810, to the designs of C. S. Smith of Warwick, opened in 1814 and reputed to have cost £30,000. There was an assembly room, reaching to the full height of the building, and 20 baths for mineral water treatments which were among the finest in the country when the Pump Rooms were first opened.

Their popularity ensured great profits for the original owners until about 1848, when the fashion of 'taking the waters' declined. After changing owners several times the building was modernised in 1861 in an effort to restore the financial success of the venture and in 1867 sold to the Local Board of Health. The Pump Rooms have been owned by the local authority ever since and have undergone various changes. In 1887 the inside was altered, a large swimming bath was built at the rear, a tower added to the front elevation, and further work was done in 1910 and 1926. The tower which featured in many old photographs was removed and the Pump Rooms restored to their former external design in 1953, to mark the Coronation of Elizabeth II.

Some of the columns seen in the photograph are the original ones of Derbyshire stone, transported from Derby by canal, but after all the alterations of the past, very little of the first building survives, although the regency appearance of the assembly room is almost unchanged and this room is now used as a restaurant.

The baths offer treatment for various rheumatic complaints, as well as all types of physiotherapy, and these are the only Pump Rooms where hydrotherapy treatment with mineral spring water is still available under the National Health Service.

1984 is the 200th anniversary of the discovery of the first mineral spring in Leamington Spa; in all seven were located, the last one in 1819. The Pump Room spring, discovered in 1810, was the sixth, and it is now the only spring still supplying spa water in the town.

The Arts Centre, University of Warwick The University of Warwick occupies a large campus of over 200 acres on the outskirts of Coventry having about 5,500 students working in modern buildings erected since the University was established in 1965.

The Arts Centre, opened in 1974, forms part of the overall plan for the development of the campus, this building having been designed by the architects Shepheard, Epstein and Hunter.

It includes a large theatre to seat over 500, a studio theatre, conference room, music centre and a bookshop as well as a major concert hall for 1,329 people. The Centre is bringing to Warwickshire some of the most important national and international orchestras and theatrical companies, all performances being open to the general public as well as to members of the University.

76

The Cathedrals, Coventry There have been three cathedrals in the city which was once the fourth most important in the kingdom. The first building was demolished at the time of the Reformation, and not until 1918 was the second cathedral dedicated when the modern diocese of Coventry was created. At that time the great medieval parish church of St Michaels became the cathedral and in November 1940 it was devastated by fire bombs, which destroyed the timber roof and the whole of the interior leaving the shattered stonework of the walls open to the sky. But the decision to rebuild was made immediately after the bombing and the now famous 'charred cross' made from two of the burnt oak beams was set up within the polygonal apse of the ruined chancel where it can still be seen above the words *Father Forgive* written there just after the destruction of the cathedral and the adjacent city centre. Then, as now, these words symbolised the gospel of reconciliation among peoples for which Coventry is famous throughout the world.

The ruined apse, seen silhouetted against the sky now appears to be rather fragile in comparison with Sir Basil Spence's new cathedral consecrated in 1962. The old cathedral is now not a mute ruin, but a place of great activity as it was when first built; then being cherished by the Guilds of medieval Coventry. The new cathedral, linked to the old by a flight of steps and a lofty porch, owes much to the talents of many modern artists and craftsmen as did the old building in its time. In the new cathedral can be seen work by John Piper, Elizabeth Frink, John Hutton, Patrick Reyntiens, Hans Coper, Margeret Traherne and many more, dominated by the magnificent tapestry of 'Christ in Glory' designed by Graham Sutherland covering the whole of the east end of the nave. Outside by the steps and behind the trees is the fine sculpture of St Michael defeating the devil, by Sir Jacob Epstein, his last major work before his death.

*City Centre from the tower of the old
cathedral, Coventry* From the tower at the
base of the spire of the old cathedral, the
view takes in a group of prewar buildings on
sites awaiting redevelopment, and
Broadgate, the square at the centre of the
reconstructed bomb-damaged Coventry.
The buildings enclosing perhaps the most
uncompromising postwar city centre were
the first to be erected in the 1950's on a
plan designed by Donald Gibson, the city
architect at that time. Broadgate leads to a
wide shopping precinct on the axis of the
old cathedral spire, terminated at the
western end by the single white tower
80 block.

Lady Godiva Statue, Coventry Leofric, Earl of Mercia, Lord of Coventry, and his wife Godiva founded and richly endowed a Benedictine monastery in Coventry before the Norman invasion. Godiva is best remembered for only one of her unselfish acts, which is here commemorated in the bronze statue by Sir William Reid Dick, erected in the centre of bomb-damaged Coventry in 1949, the gift of W. H. Bassett-Green, a local businessman.

Godiva's persistent pleas for relaxation of the heavy taxes imposed on the townsfolk by Leofric were answered by his challenge that she should ride naked before the people in the market place. This done, the Earl kept his part of the bargain, and now the bronze Godiva surveys Broadgate, site of the streets through which she rode. The citizens of Coventry still applaud a modern Godiva who rides in the annual carnival procession, maintaining a custom which was known to have started during the Coventry fair of 1678, if not earlier, and although it has sometimes lapsed it has been revived to continue to the present day.

The statue was erected to mark the heart of the new city centre started immediately after the war. It was one of the first things to rise in bomb-scarred Coventry marking a faith in its future. Now surrounded by less attractive planting, it originally formed the centrepiece of a garden bright with bulbs presented to the citizens of Coventry by the people of the Netherlands as a token of friendship in the difficult years after the war.

Bedworth Parish Church Bedworth, an ancient settlement in north-east Warwickshire, had become firmly established as a mining centre by the end of the 17th century and is now part of the Warwickshire coalfield district. The church originally dated from the 15th century, and resembled many built in the country about that time, but all that remains of the old church is the tower, with a bell that has been ringing since the days of Cromwell. The rest of the church of All Saints was rebuilt in 1888–90 by Bodley and Garner, except for the old tower with its 1817 clock, which were both known to Mary Ann Evans, better known as George Eliot the novelist, who was born in 1819 at Arbury Farm. She lived there until 1841 when she moved to Coventry.

In the churchyard are many slate headstones with fine incised inscriptions, examples of the art of ornamental lettering practised by the masons of the 18th and early 19th centuries.

Town Centre, Bedworth A view of a new shopping area built in 1970 as part of Bedworth's Market Street redevelopment, changing the face of this old town, the centre of a long established coal mining area in which the first pit was sunk in the 17th century. The peak of mining activity came during the period 1870 to 1914 when the town expanded rapidly, and now because of the recent closure of the neighbouring mines the character of the town and its industries has started to change as other types of businesses move into the district.

Not far away, Mary Ann Evans (George Eliot) lived with her father who was agent for the Newdigate family of Arbury Hall. The Newdigates owned one of the first mines in the district, now worked out. George Eliot's town has almost vanished from sight after the construction of modern roads, factories, and the new civic and shopping centre, but she would still recognise the sound of Bedworth's voices.

Arbury Hall, near Nuneaton Arbury Hall remains the most complete example of the 18th century 'Gothic Revival' in the country. It is part of a house built by Richard Newdigate about 1670 on the site of an older house. In 1750, with the help of Sanderson Miller of Radway Grange, Sir Roger Newdigate, the fifth baronet, began 'gothicising' the house, and the interior plasterwork is some of the finest of its kind found in any English country house.

Mary Ann Evans (George Eliot), knew the house well and used it as her model for Cheveral Manor in *Scenes of Clerical Life* written in 1857, Sir Roger Newdigate appearing in the character of Sir Christopher Cheveral.

Rugby School A view of the heart of the famous public school at Rugby, with the tower of its chapel silhouetted against the sky.

This school, founded in 1567 as a free grammar school to serve the children of Rugby and Brownsover, is now an independent public school of international reputation. The first buildings on the present site were erected between 1809 and 1816, when the School House, Old Quad and the original chapel were built. During the time of Dr Arnold (1828-1842) it became and still remains one of the largest schools of its kind in the country.

No buildings earlier than 1800 survive and many of the existing buildings are late Victorian, including the large and impressive chapel built in 1872 to designs by William Butterfield. Its central octagonal tower with a steep pyramid-shaped roof and gargoyles is constructed in polychrome patterned brickwork of a type much admired today thanks to the modern reappraisal of Victorian architecture.

Made famous in literature by *Tom Brown's Schooldays* and in sport by William Webb Ellis who in 1823 reinterpreted the rules of football, remembering Rupert Brooke among its famous pupils, the school has demonstrated the resilience of its tradition by making the senior forms co-educational a few years ago.

Dunchurch A group of thatched and brick-built cottages at Dunchurch, alongside the road from Rugby which leads into the centre of this old village. These cottages are like many of the dwellings built for farm workers in the last century and now modernised to become desirable homes. Many had later brick fronts concealing the original timber framework which may often still be seen inside, or hiding the clay walls typical of the poorer houses of the period. These are a few which have survived from the 19th century despite the growth of neighbouring Rugby which has now almost engulfed the old village.

Dunchurch is near the eastern boundary of Warwickshire and one of the few villages astride this part of the A45, because other ancient settlements were built just off this road across Dunsmore Heath, described in 1675 by Ogilby, the famous mapmaker, as 'notoriously bad'. Traditionally the home of the Dun Cow slain by the legendary Guy of Warwick it was later the haunt of highway-men. This road through the centre of the village was the original coach road from London to Chester, improved by Thomas Telford early in the last century as a route to Holyhead and thence to Ireland and now the modern A45 is in its turn bypassed by the M45 motorway which starts not far away.

92

Guy Fawkes House, Dunchurch A glimpse of the perpendicular style tower of St Peter's church, built in local red sandstone, is seen beyond the former Lion Inn, with its close vertical timber-framing and its jettied or overhanging upper floor. Although restored, the building is largely of 16th century origin, a fine building long ago divided into houses one of which is named Guy Fawkes House, as on 6 November 1605 at the invitation of Sir Everard Digby, a number of Warwickshire catholic gentry met at the inn for supper after spending the

day hunting on the neighbouring Dunsmore Heath. They awaited news of the success of the Gunpowder Plot which they had organised but Robert Catesby, who had ridden 80 miles from London in seven hours, brought news of the failure of the Plot and the arrest of Guy Fawkes. Many of the plotters fled by way of Warwick, Snitterfield and Great Alne into Worcestershire where they were later apprehended; so ended what later generations called 'The bloody hunting match at Dunchurch'.

Parish Church, Southam St James' Church was built on the high ground overlooking the valley of the small river Itchen, and it still stands on the edge of the town's market square as it has done for the last 600 years. The red sandstone and lias church was built in the 15th century with its large chancel and aisles as well as the nave with its fine carved timber roof admired by worshippers and visitors alike, although much of the interior was altered during the various restorations carried out during the reign of Queen Victoria and later. The west tower with its 120ft high broach spire contains a fine peal of bells which were silent when Charles I visited the town in 1641. For this neglect the doors of the church were locked by the King's men, who had to be bribed to reopen them, the payment being recorded in the Churchwarden's account book for that year.

The people of Southam must also have heard the fighting at the nearby hamlet of Bascote when on 23 August 1642 the first engagement of the Civil War took place between the Royalist troops and those, under Lord Brooke of Warwick Castle, who fought for Parliament. In the skirmish the King lost 50 men and some cannon before setting out to Nottingham where he raised his Standard on 25 August. In the same year the King stayed the night in Southam at the 16th century manor house in the main street before the Battle of Edgehill. This timber framed house, partly covered with rendering, stands on the corner of the road to Daventry and is now used as a chemist's shop.

Southam also had its moments of glory in the past when Augustine Bernher was rector at the church in the reign of Mary Stuart. During the persecutions of the martyrs, Latimer, Ridley and Cramer, he acted as their servant just before they were burnt at the stake. How Bernher himself escaped a similar fate is a mystery. A little while later, Shakespeare obviously knew the town as it is mentioned in Act V, Sc I of Henry VI, part III, when Warwick the Kingmaker, awaiting his army, is told by Sir John Somerville that Clarence is not far away 'At Southam I did leave him with his forces And do expect him here some two hours hence'.

96

Napton Canal Locks The 'Napton Flight' of locks is on the original Oxford Canal — since 1 January 1929 part of the Grand Union Canal system — runs around Napton-on-the-Hill before descending a long flight of locks to lower ground on its route south towards Banbury, Oxford, the Thames and London.

Originally intended to take narrow boats it was constructed in the 20 years following the passing of the Act of Parliament to build the canal in 1769. It later became part of the Grand Junction Canal system and has been progressively widened since it was incorporated into the Grand Union Canal.

This attractive view shows some of the many boats using the canal moored near the boat yard and the waterside public house alongside a typical humped-back bridge used along this canal. Beyond can be seen the tree and hedge lined route of the canal as it wanders through low lying countryside on the eastern fringes of the county, an area of mixed farming, small villages, and a number of deserted medieval village sites.

Restoring the Windmill at Napton, Warwickshire Napton Windmill has been a landmark for generations of travellers along the Southam to Daventry road, once part of an old stage coach route, now much used by modern traffic. The windmill stands high on a hill almost 500ft above the undulating surrounding countryside and from which there are fine views over the Warwickshire landscape bordering Northamptonshire.

Napton is the Anglo-Saxon name for 'a village on a hill' and is the only example of a hillside village in Warwickshire. It has always been a comparatively large place, having over a hundred houses in 1730, and clings around the east and south of the hill, some distance from the windmill which stands half-a-mile WNW of the ancient parish church on the western edge of the hill.

The mill was built about 1835, ceased milling in 1909, and was almost abandoned until repairs started in 1972. Work has continued although much remains to be done to make good the loss of the sails which were destroyed in a storm not so many years ago.

This mill is the survivor of a pair of windmills which stood near one another, the older mill built before 1725 being demolished some time towards the end of the last century. The present windmill is one of about 50 which were intact in Warwickshire at the start of the present century, of which only 17 are now extant, almost all converted into houses or used for purposes other than the grinding of corn.

Farnborough Hall near Warmington Farnborough Hall was given to the National Trust just after the last war by the Holbech family who had owned it since Ambrose Holbech purchased the property in 1684. It was he who altered the existing house, building the brown ironstone-faced wing shown in the photograph and landscaping the site. He was perhaps responsible for planting some of the magnificent trees including the Cedars of Lebanon for which the gardens are well known and also for the spectacular terrace walk from which fine views westwards are obtained across the narrow valley towards Warmington and beyond to Edgehill. This terrace, laid out on the side of the hill on which the hall stands, was designed by Sanderson Miller who lived a few miles away at Radway Grange; along the walk are a simple Ionic temple, an 18th century domed oval pavilion with Tuscan columns and a rococo plastered interior, and at the end the focal point is an obelisk first erected in 1751, but since rebuilt. Below the terrace three lakes were formed by damming a stream, the largest being Sourland Pool, a peaceful setting for this lovely old house. It may be disturbed for all time for through this narrow valley, a mile or two wide, road engineers plan to construct the M40, Birmingham to Oxford motorway.

The Hall is open from April to September and is famous for the magnificent 18th century rococo style interior plasterwork. The entrance hall, decorated in Etruscan red, has elaborate plasterwork niches containing the busts of emperors, but perhaps the finest room is the dining room with a white marble chimney piece and a plasterwork over mantel surrounding a view of the Capitol at Rome. Upstairs the Chinese room is decorated in the chinoiserie style of the period. All this is to be seen inside an 18th century building of brick with stone quoins, with an entrance elevation built about 1750, nine bays wide with projecting side wings. The stone facade, seven bays wide, as seen in the photograph, facing towards the garden was built slightly earlier.

Kineton This old monument is a focal point among the houses forming continuous road frontages which give Kineton so much of its character. The village is a settlement of great antiquity 10 miles south-east of Warwick situated on the banks of the river Dene as recorded in Norman times. Though now considered to be a village it was once a medieval market town of some importance a role it maintained until 1840 when the market house was pulled down.

The charm of Kineton lies in its wide streets and variety of its old buildings, many built in the dark red local brick or the brown Hornton and grey lias stones of the district, some date from the 17th century although a few older buildings may be detected by the observant. A feature of the village is

St Peter's church, originally built in the 13th and 15th centuries, but thanks to later and drastic restorations of 1755 and 1885 the present church is largely of those years. The perpendicular style tower and the Early English west door however escaped the worst attentions of the restorers.

In the last century Kineton became an important agricultural centre, and recently has expanded offering houses for commuters to the larger towns in the neighbourhood, with factories on a small industrial estate providing some local employment.

Kineton probably changed very little in the period from 23 October 1642, when the first battle of the Civil War took place at Edgehill, until the last war. The famous

battle took place about three miles to the south-east just inside the parish, and the streets of Kineton were then crowded with the horses and wagons of the 'Roundheads' under Lord Essex who were trying to intercept the King's March from Worcester to London.

Looking down on the Battlefield of 1642, Edgehill A panoramic view from the Edgehill escarpment, one of the highest points in the county, above the village of Radway across the undulating countryside of the Warwickshire 'Feldon' northwards towards the Avon valley, the towers of Warwick Castle, the high buildings of modern Coventry and westwards towards the Malvern Hills. In the immediate vicinity, beyond Radway village hidden behind the trees, is a prosperous area of mixed farming. Apart from the enclosed fields, the different crops, and modern farm buildings, the landscape below the ridge can have changed very little since 23 October 1642 when King Charles I stood looking down at the opposing armies in the fields between Radway and Kineton, visible in the distance.

On the ridge stands Edgehill Tower, erected in the 18th century by Sanderson Miller (who lived at Radway Grange, seen in the centre of the photograph) to mark the spot where it is assumed that the King's Standard was raised before he descended the steep hill to engage the Parliamentary forces.

It was on these low lying fields that the first major battle of the Civil War was fought, an inconclusive battle still remembered today though many more important battles of the same period are often forgotten. On these gentle fields many hundreds of Englishmen died fighting on both sides for a cause they believed in, and the survivors buried many of the dead where they lay while others were placed in the churchyard at Radway. Even today relics of the battle are sometimes unearthed by modern deep ploughing on local farmland. The spire of the church built at Radway in 1866 can be seen above the trees surrounding the village and contains the monument, with a reclining effigy, of Captain Henry Kingsmill who was killed during the battle. The monument was moved from the original church, long since demolished, where the people must have heard and seen the fighting in progress while attending morning service.

Upton House Upton House, in fine landscaped grounds, stands on the top of Edge Hill on the site of a village depopulated in 1499 and not far from the village of Tysoe. The house is near the top of Sunrising Hill, which did not acquire this romantic name until about 1725, and looks out over that part of south Warwickshire traditionally known as 'the Vale of the Red Horse' because of the figure which was cut out of the grass on the side of the hill to expose the red soil underneath. All traces of 'The Red Horse' have now been lost. It was destroyed in 1798 at the enclosure of the open fields of the parish, although opinions differ as to what the figure represented. Some say it was associated with the heathen god of war, Tiw, who gave his name to the ancient village of Tysoe, the word meaning 'Tiw's hill', but others prefer to believe that the figure was carved in memory of Richard Neville, Warwick the Kingmaker, who to encourage the army at the Battle of Towton in 1461, slew his horse and fought alongside his men rather than retreat.

Whatever the truth, Upton House stands where Sunrising Hill rises up from the undulating Feldon of south Warwickshire to the plateau at the top of Edge Hill and out of the Midland Plain into the high land of Oxfordshire and to the Thames Valley beyond. Parts of the house date from the 15th century, but most of it is 17th century and later; the main fronts being built in 1695 although some alterations were made in the 1730s by Sanderson Miller, the amateur architect and garden designer, who lived not far away at Radway Grange. Further down the hill, in the gardens, are the Temple Pool and a Tuscan temple, a feature of the landscape gardens he designed at the time he also 'improved' the house.

In 1757 the house was purchased by Robert Child, the banker, whose daughter Sarah Anne eloped with the Earl of Westmorland who married her at Gretna Green. The house was left to Robert Child's grand-daughter who became the wife of the 5th Earl of Jersey. The estate remained the property of Earl of Jersey's descendants until purchased in this century by Viscount Bearsted, who gave the house to the National Trust in 1948. The house is open to the public.

108

Compton Wynyates Compton Wynyates, about 12 miles south-east of Stratford-upon-Avon, is all that remains of the village of Compton depopulated by Sir William Compton in the reign of Henry VIII to enable the park around his new house to be created. The house belonging to the Marquess of Northampton is among the best preserved Tudor houses in the country; although being the home of the Marquess and his family it has in recent years not been open to the public, much to the regret of visitors. The mansion, lying in a fold of the escarpment of Edge Hill close to the Oxfordshire border, takes its name from Compton — 'a settlement in a dale or hollow', while Wynyates probably derives from the word for 'a vineyard'.

The manor first came into the possession of Philip de Compton about 1204 and has been owned ever since by the same family, one of the oldest of the County families and one of the very few to hold their houses continuously for so long. In 1618 the 2nd Lord Compton was created an Earl by James I and in 1812 the 9th Earl was made a Marquess which title is still held by the family.

The original moated house was pulled down and a new brick and stone house started about 1481 by Edmund de Compton, part of which still survives around the courtyard of the present house. His son was knighted by Henry VIII after the Battle of Tournai in 1512 and the king also gave him the old castle at Fulbroke, near Warwick. This was demolished to provide materials for enlarging the house at Compton Wynyates and creating the mansion that still exists. It is known that the timber roof of the hall and probably the oriel window facing the courtyard came from Fulbroke, and some bricks were no doubt made on the site with the clay dug out of the moat as the remains of old brick kilns have been found near the long pond. The colour range of the hand-made bricks is vast, with hardly two bricks being the same shade; ranging from pale rose, through orange to dark red and blue, these being used for the diaper work typical of the period creating what Pevsner describes as 'the most perfect picture-book house of the Early Tudor decades'. Henry VIII stayed here several times, probably with Catherine of Aragon, as did Elizabeth I, James I and

Charles I.

List of Plates

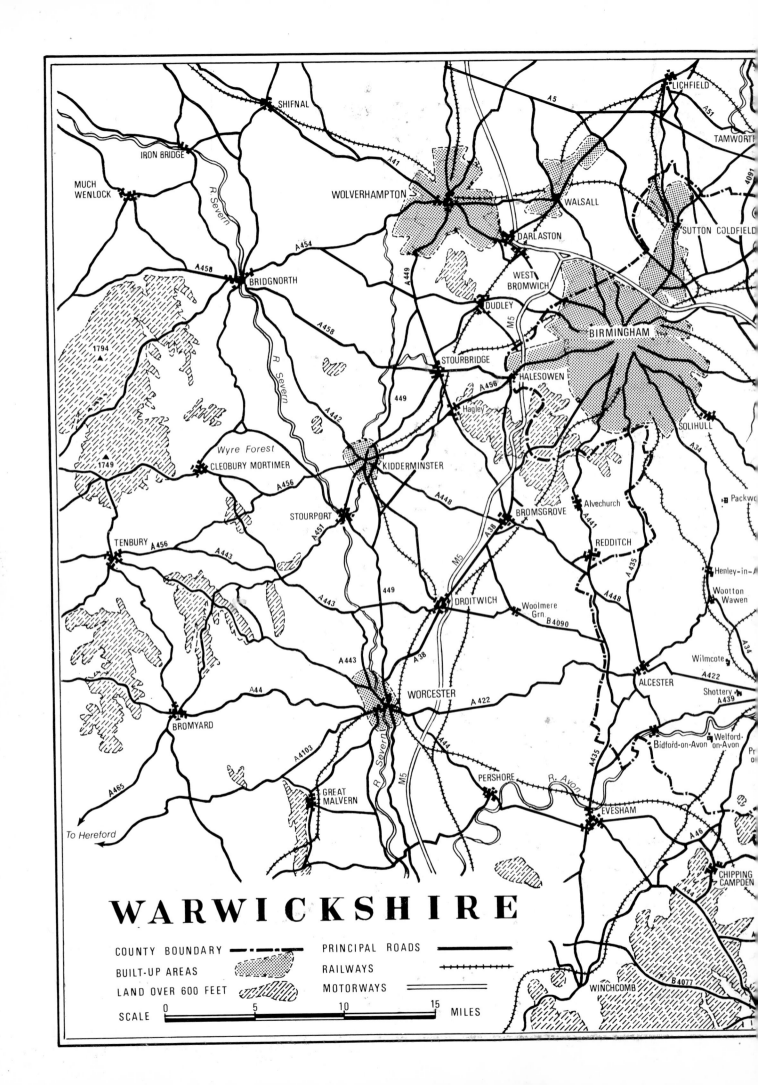

WARWICKSHIRE

COUNTY BOUNDARY
BUILT-UP AREAS
LAND OVER 600 FEET

PRINCIPAL ROADS
RAILWAYS
MOTORWAYS

SCALE 0   5   10   15   MILES